First Facts®

Best of Pro Sports

The
Best of
Pro Basketball

First Facts is published by Capstone Press,
151 Good Counsel Drive, P.O. Box 669, Mankato, Minnesota 56002.
www.capstonepub.com

 Books published by Capstone Press are manufactured with paper
containing at least 10 percent post-consumer waste.

Library of Congress Cataloging-in-Publication Data
Doeden, Matt.
    The best of pro basketball / by Matt Doeden.
    p. cm. — (First facts. Best of pro sports)
    Includes bibliographical references and index.
    Summary: "Presents some of the best moments and players in professional basketball
history" — Provided by publisher.
    ISBN 978-1-4296-3332-1 (library binding)
    ISBN 978-1-4296-3880-7 (softcover)
    1. Basketball — United States — History — Juvenile literature. 2. Basketball players
— United States — History — Juvenile literature. I. Title. II. Series.
GV885.1.D63 2010
796.323'640973 — dc22   2009001174

Table of Contents

Best Scorer...4

Most Points
   by a Player in a Game 7

Best Shootout 8

Best Comeback 10

Best Rebounder 12

Best Steal 14

Best Last-Second Shot 16

Most Amazing Shot.............................19

Best Three-Point Shooter 20

Glossary 22
Read More..23
Internet Sites 23
Index...24

Best Scorer

Michael Jordan was a scoring machine. He could hit shots inside or outside the three-point line. In 15 seasons, he scored 32,292 points. He won a record 10 scoring titles. His talent for scoring helped the Chicago Bulls win six NBA titles in the 1990s.

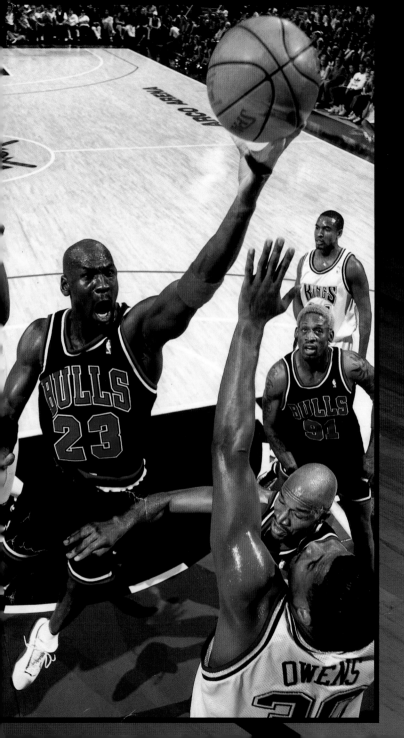

Runner-up

Nobody in the NBA scored more points than Kareem Abdul-Jabbar. In 20 NBA seasons, he scored 38,387 points. He scored more points than Jordan, but he also played five more seasons.

Most Points by a Player in a Game

In the NBA, 20 points for one player is a good night. Thirty points marks a great night. But what about scoring 100 points in one game? It sounds impossible, but Wilt Chamberlain did it. On March 2, 1962, he destroyed his old record of 78 points. What a player!

Best Shootout

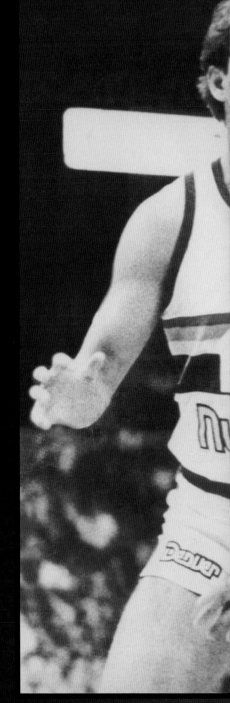

Imagine scoring 184 points in a game and still losing! It happened to the Denver Nuggets on December 13, 1983. The Nuggets and Detroit Pistons traded baskets at a blistering pace. The game was tied 145-145 at the end of the fourth quarter. Three overtimes later, Detroit ended it with a 186-184 victory.

Best Comeback

It was game four of the 2008 NBA Finals. The Boston Celtics were in trouble. The Los Angeles Lakers had an early 24-point lead. But the Celtics didn't give up. They cut the lead to 18 points by halftime. In the second half, they outscored the Lakers 57-33. The Celtics came back to win 97-91.

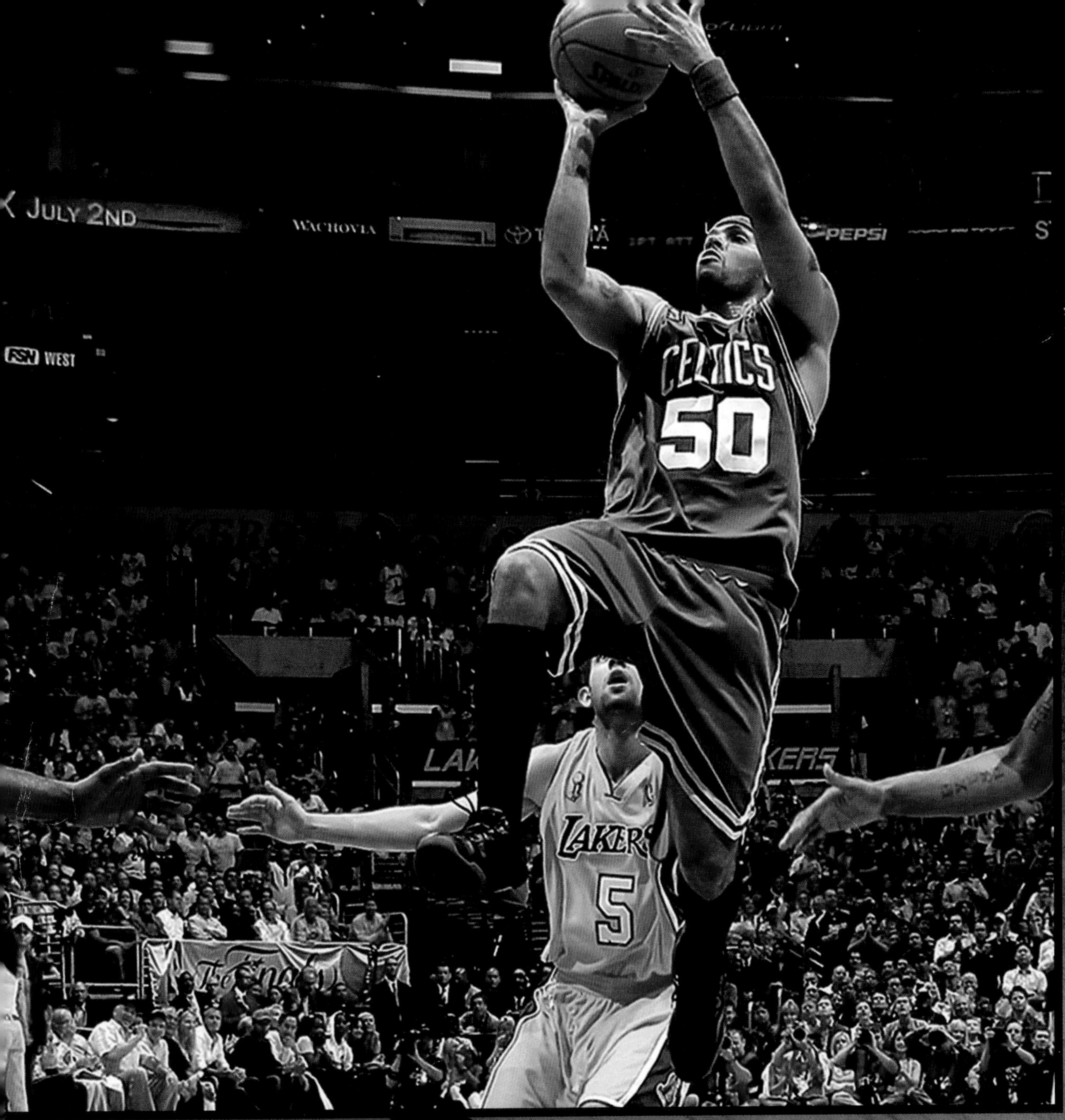
JULY 2ND
WACHOVIA
PEPSI
FSN WEST
CELTICS
50
LAKERS
5

Best Rebounder

Wilt Chamberlain was a beast on the backboards. From 1959 to 1974, he had a record 23,924 **rebounds**. He holds the record of 55 rebounds in a game. His best season for rebounds was 1960-1961. He had an **average** of 27.2 rebounds per game.

rebound: the act of gaining possession of the ball after a missed shot

average: a number found by adding all rebounds made and dividing by the number of games played

Runner-up

Boston's Bill Russell had 21,620 rebounds in his 13-year career. He had an average of 22.5 rebounds per game.

Best Steal

Only six seconds remained in a 1987 playoff game. The Detroit Pistons led the Boston Celtics by one point. Detroit's Isiah Thomas made an inbound pass. But Boston's Larry Bird stole it away. He quickly passed the ball to Dennis Johnson. Johnson knocked down the winning shot. The Celtics went on to win the series.

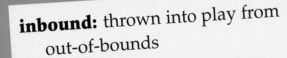

inbound: thrown into play from out-of-bounds

Larry Bird

Runner-up

Celtic John Havlicek made a similar steal in the 1965 playoffs. Philadelphia needed a basket to tie the game. But Havlicek stole the inbound pass. He dished it to teammate Sam Jones for the winning basket.

Best Last-Second Shot

It was game six of the 1998 NBA Finals. The Utah Jazz led the Chicago Bulls by one point. Michael Jordan had the ball near mid-court. He started to drive hard to his right. Then he quickly stopped, shedding his defender. He jumped and knocked down one of the greatest shots in NBA history. The shot gave Chicago its sixth NBA title.

Is It a Tie?

In the 2004 playoffs, the San Antonio Spurs led the Los Angeles Lakers. Less than half a second remained to play. Guard Derek Fisher took the inbound pass for the Lakers. He shot the ball as it hit his hands. He released the winning shot as the buzzer sounded. What a finish!

Most Amazing Shot

In the 1980 NBA Finals, Julius Erving went up for a baseline shot. But Kareem Abdul-Jabbar was ready to block it. Erving shifted his body and soared behind the backboard. He reached his long arm around the backboard and tossed in a reverse layup. The shot is known simply as "The Move."

baseline: the out-of-bounds line on either end of a basketball court

layup: a close shot where the ball is gently played off the backboard and into the hoop

Best Three-Point Shooter

Nobody could shoot three-pointers like the Indiana Pacers' Reggie Miller. In his 18-year career, he made a record 2,560 three-point shots. He holds the record of 320 three-pointers in the playoffs. Miller's best season was 1996-1997. He made 229 three-point shots that season.

Glossary

average (AV-uh-rij) — a number found by adding all rebounds made and dividing by the number of games played

baseline (BAYSS-line) — the out-of-bounds line on either end of a basketball court

inbound (IN-bound) — thrown into play from out-of-bounds

layup (LAY-up) — a close shot where the ball is gently played off the backboard and into the hoop

playoff (PLAY-awf) — a series of games played after the regular season to decide a championship

rebound (REE-bound) — the act of gaining possession of the ball after a missed shot

Read More

Doeden, Matt. *The Greatest Basketball Records.* Sports Records. Mankato, Minn.: Capstone Press, 2009.

Giglio, Joe. *Great Teams in Pro Basketball History.* Great Teams. Chicago: Raintree, 2006.

Stewart, Mark, and Mike Kennedy. *Swish: The Quest for Basketball's Perfect Shot.* Minneapolis: Millbrook Press, 2009.

Internet Sites

FactHound offers a safe, fun way to find Internet sites related to this book. All of the sites on FactHound have been researched by our staff.

Here's all you do:

Visit *www.facthound.com*

FactHound will fetch the best sites for you!

Abdul-Jabbar, Kareem, 5, 19

Bird, Larry, 14

Chamberlain, Wilt, 7, 12
comebacks, 10

Erving, Julius, 19

Fisher, Derek, 17

Havlicek, John, 15

Johnson, Dennis, 14
Jones, Sam, 15
Jordan, Michael, 4, 5, 16

last-second shots, 16, 17

Miller, Reggie, 20

NBA Finals, 10, 16, 19

overtime, 8

playoffs, 10, 14, 15, 16, 17,
    19, 20

rebounds, 12, 13
Russell, Bill, 13

scoring, 4, 5, 7, 8, 10, 20
shootouts, 8
steals, 14, 15

Thomas, Isiah, 14
three-point shots, 20